Brian A. Wilson

THE TRAUMA OF THE BLACK MAN IN AMERICA

© The Trauma of the Black Man in America

A letter from the author:
At this time, America is at a reckoning of its prior solemn dutiful service to its citizens to mark up a nation's stain of glory. My goal and duty to the American people are to set forth a bleaching tale of a country onward to the glory of righteous faith. Solemn in mind and oath, I embark you on a necessary pilgrimage into the American Soul-Nation of a land and its beauty. The purpose of this tale is to set forth America in its righteousness and abridge America in its separation of dutiful goals. The premise here is to reshape the tale of justice as a story of bravery and the truth of its present narrative of nationhood. The story here is of a kind heritage - a retelling of a nation outlined in its glory. The book The Trauma of the Black Man in America is not a rehash of the United States of America civil war of the 1840s; this book is a nod forward from the 1990s onward into modern history.

Brian A. Wilson
B.A. History, (The) University of Memphis
BrianAuthorWilson@aol.com
HISTORIAN_BRIANWILSON **Instagram**
HISTORIAN BRIAN A WILSON **Facebook**

Prepare to be whisked away into a foreign but close and even right-at-home country heritage of a story of justice at the porch of the face of our community.

The Trauma of the Black Man in America

Problem: Addressing the Trauma of the American Black Man
Solution: Royal Regeneration of the American Soul-Nation

You are now whisked away in the conundrum of the Black Man in America.

Author Notes: Focus: Soul-Nation, a collective functionality of American modern history
through the eyes of an American quandary - a true pledge of allegorical allegiance as the Black Man in America.

I AM THANKFUL TO THE ONES WHO INSPIRED THIS BOOK.

ABOUT THE AUTHOR

Brian A. Wilson is a renowned historian and author known for his extensive research and insightful analysis of the experiences and struggles of the Black community in America. With a deep passion for unraveling the intricacies of history, Wilson has dedicated his career to shedding light on the trauma faced by Black men throughout American history. His groundbreaking work, "The Trauma of the Black Man in America," explores the multifaceted and deeply rooted traumas that have shaped the Black male experience, examining the historical, social, and psychological factors at play.

Brian grew up in Memphis, Tennessee garnering a firmness of purpose for social justice and change. Wilson's meticulous research and empathetic approach provide readers with a comprehensive understanding of the lasting impact of systemic racism, violence, and discrimination on the lives of Black men. Through his compelling storytelling and thought-provoking analysis, Wilson challenges prevailing narratives and invites readers to confront uncomfortable truths about the history of racial oppression in America. As a highly respected historian, Wilson's work has been widely recognized and celebrated, making him an influential voice in the field of African American studies. Brian "The" Historian's commitment to unearthing marginalized histories and amplifying the voices of the oppressed has accumulated him both critical acclaim and a dedicated following. With "The Trauma of the Black Man in America," Brian A. Wilson continues to contribute to the ongoing dialogue surrounding race, providing invaluable insights that are necessary for a more inclusive society.

A journey into

Chapter 1: American Pain
Chapter 2: Servitude
Chapter 3: American Idealism
Chapter 4: Where does the Black Man fit in American Society
Chapter 5: Family - A Juxtapositional Reality
Chapter 6: Wholeness - Exploring the Togetherness of the American Spirit
Chapter 7: A Grapple with American Crime
Chapter 8: Governmental Law - A Momentous Comparison of Laws Affecting Black Men
Chapter 9: Equal Justice Under the Law

Chapter 10: Inflection Point - Navigating the Turning Tide of Trauma and Hope

Chapter 11: Black Heritage

Chapter 12: Recompense

Chapter 13: Human Consciousness Is Rising

Chapter 14: American Closure

Chapter 15: George Washington's Warning to the State: Upholding American Liberty for its Citizens

CHAPTER 1

AMERICAN PAIN

"A look back to early America."

The pain starts with the realization that, as a black man, others might see him as a threat. When the black man leaves his home, he may not meet suspicious glares and anxious looks from people who might assume the black man is up to no good. He could be walking to the store, jogging in your neighborhood, or playing at the park, but to some; he is suspect.

The constant fear of violence compounds the deep-rooted and even elevated levels of pain tied to the tree of social injustices in the heartland of North America. The headlines are in a world filled with tales of black men killed by police officers who are supposed to protect and serve. The names of George Floyd, Breonna Taylor, and Ahmaud Arbery have become synonymous with the daily fear and trauma black men may face; it is a pain that is passed down from generation to generation, a tale of ancestors who may have been enslaved, lynched, and discriminated against still echo in our hearts. We carry the burden of their trauma, which might add to our own.

Many black men felt pain in the workplace; Black men face discrimination regarding hiring and promotions. The trauma of being a black man in America is not just physical, but it is also psychological. The constant micro-aggressions, the subtle snubs, and the overt discrimination can take a toll on a man's mental health. Depression, post-traumatic stress disorder (PTSD), and anxiety are just some mental health issues that black men face.

We live in a society that seems to value whiteness and punishes Blackness. The trauma of being a black man in America is a pain that is always present, and it is one that we cannot ignore. We must acknowledge it, confront it, and work towards healing ourselves and our communities. The pain is real, but so is our resilience. We have survived centuries of oppression and will continue fighting for justice and equality. Our pain may be The United States of America's, our society's shame, but it is also our strength.

One cannot forget the efficient tail of darker-skinned enslaved individuals whose captains transported from the developments of Colonial land east of the continent of North America.

Traveling back to the world's uncertain morals in an assertion of Black Slavery would be a disservice to the concept of this book. The American story of pain starts here - neglect of the right or wrong side of Black Slavery. America is young, and our lady is with wonder and excitement about our new home. A brittle bunch - heroes through and through will begin our story.

Black men in America were forced into the solid Southern willful demand to join the American Civil War to fight or rather die for a cause yet determined. Scholars would assert that the Black man is honorable - entering into American-caused history has been deemed worthy of the fights. The Black man in America began in a battle for himself. He started in a less than favorable position to admonish our country's war efforts and for the American cause. In a fit of clandestine heroism, the black man stood tall to fulfill his new American duty to join the war effort. In his chest, it stung of a solicited hope to one day be an acceptable citizen of birth of an American Black Man. With his chest held up high - he marches. The Black man strides into the hopeful calamity of a nation, notwithstanding its determination to fulfill a God-Given prophecy. How painful it might have been to dredge into an American cause that only a God force could subdue, so we fight. The Black man was of two minds history would prove trampled down head-on - soldiers in a time bit that would charge American values forward - her[America] willfully awaiting her destiny.

■■

CHAPTER 2

SERVITUDE

Our American countrymen in his service do the great work in and of justice in service himself the nation of a resounding glimmer of American causations. Man's countenance, in his way, is that of service. Service is to his God in that he may deem his savior as a duty to men or as that of a holy cause. The Black man carries an unspoken servanthood to that of his dutiful countenance of service to thy brother. What is the service to thy fellow but one that will at any cause advance the move forward as a demand of sacrifice? The Black man, as himself a brother of men, seeks to dredge himself as a continuum in the valor of distinct as he embraces a cause of causes that intertwined into his very destiny. In an ode to the fathers of its time, America, a nation of brethren, recognizes the path it must lay to satisfy an elusive forecast of bravery in a country built on the premise of a free man.

The unspoken duty of the Black man in America is a complex notion of service ingrained in the Black community throughout history. We explore how the Black man's sense of duty and sacrifice has shaped his identity and contributed to the collective pursuit of justice. The intertwining threads of servanthood, sacrifice, and brotherhood are an insight into Black men's unique experiences and challenges as they strive to fulfill their destinies in a nation built on the promise of freedom.

The Black man is our American countryman serving America as a testament to the great work carried out to pursue justice. Through his steadfast commitment to equality and fairness, the Black man plays an essential role in shaping the nation's identity and progress. In the face of adversity, he has dedicated himself to uplifting his community and challenging the systemic barriers that hinder true justice for all.

Service is inherent to man's countenance in his way, and for the Black man, it takes on a unique significance. Whether seen as a duty to his fellow men or as a holy cause, the Black man's service is rooted in his connection to a higher power. Through this unwavering dedication, he seeks to bring about positive change and pave the way for a better future.

Despite enduring centuries of oppression and marginalization, the Black man remains steadfast in his commitment to uplift and support his community; this servanthood is not born out of subservience or weakness but rather from a place of strength, resilience, and an unwavering belief in the power of unity and collective progress. Service to one's fellow man necessitates sacrifice to advance the cause, and the Black man understands this truth all too well. He embraces the challenges and hardships of striving for justice, recognizing that progress often requires personal sacrifice. Through his unwavering commitment to the cause, the Black man paves the way for a brighter future for himself and future generations, for it is up to us to do better since we know better. In the face of ill luck, he seeks to forge a path of valor and distinction, upholding the principles upon which America persists. He recognizes that his struggle for justice is not only for himself but also for the collective betterment of society.

In another ode to the founding fathers and the ideals they espoused, America must acknowledge the Black man's vital role in advancing the nation's pursuit of justice. As a nation of brethren, America has to recognize and embrace the sacrifices and contributions of the Black man. Doing so is fulfilled the elusive forecast of bravery and honors the legacy of freedom. The Black man has had a profound sense of duty, sacrifice, and brotherhood that defines the Black man's experience. The Black man has played a vital role in advancing America through his unwavering commitment to service. As the nation strives for true equality and freedom, it ought to recognize and honor the contributions of Black men, ensuring their destiny with the fabric of the nation's identity.

■■

CHAPTER 3

AMERICAN IDEALISM

The Black man is now an American ideal. Throughout history, he has fought valiantly for his rights, demanding justice and equality in a nation that has often failed to recognize his worth. Today, the Black man might symbolize resilience, strength, and the ongoing struggle for true freedom. As an American ideal, the Black man carries the weight of representation, tasked with dispelling the misconceptions and stereotypes that have plagued his community for far too long; a burden that the Black Man bears willingly, understanding the importance of setting forth an earnest reality that all Black men in America are not the same. In the eyes of the world, the American Black man is a fortifying patriot. He stands shoulder to shoulder with his brethren, ready to march forward as the United States of America extends its arms to embrace the global community. With a sense of moral duty, he becomes a Godsend, a beacon of hope in a world desperately needing harmony and understanding.

However, the Black man is not immune to the hardships that plague his community. He bore the faces of the harsh realities of systemic racism, discrimination, and inequality. Despite his best efforts, he might be entangled in a web of prejudice, often reduced to a single soul bewildered by the injustices he encounters.

Yet, the American Black man does not succumb to bitterness or despair. Instead, he rises above, recognizing his power to effect change. The Black man refuses to let the negative actions of a few define the character of an entire diaspora. In the face of adversity, he strives to mend himself, rise above the stereotypes, and prove an existence not defined by crime or wrongdoing. Nevertheless, America often fails to distinguish between these Black men; it lumps all Black men together, disregarding the incredible diversity within the Black community. By doing so, the U.S. might not serve the greater good, missing out on the wealth of talent, knowledge, and potential within the Black population.

The American Black man, with all his complexities, yearns for a society that sees him as an individual that recognizes his unique struggles and triumphs. He longs for a nation that embraces diversity within its borders, celebrating the richness that comes from accepting and valuing every citizen's contribution.

The Black Man is not an idea of your imagination nor a figment of your creation. He is an ideal steadfast, born into a nation that must celebrate but stifled his existence. He is a part of the manufactured countenance of the United States of the American soul, a complex tapestry woven with the threads of struggle and triumph.

In the landscape of American idealism, the Black Man's presence is both undeniable and indispensable. His contributions to the nation's growth, culture, and progress are immeasurable. From the earliest days of this great nation, he stood tall alongside his fellow men, working tirelessly to build a society founded on the principles of freedom and justice for all.

Yet, throughout history, the Black Man has borne witness to the contradictions within the American dream. He has experienced the harsh realities of systemic racism, discrimination, and the devaluation of his very humanity. He has faced adversity with unwavering strength, navigating a labyrinth of prejudice and injustice that seeks to confine him to the margins of society.

The Black Man refuses to be defined by the limitations imposed upon him. He rises above adversity, embracing his heritage and using it as a source of empowerment. He draws strength from his ancestry, his culture, and the unwavering spirit of his forefathers who fought for freedom and equality. In the face of the manufactured countenance of the American soul, the Black Man stands resolute. He refuses to be silenced or erased from the narrative. He demands sight, hearing, and value as integral to this nation's fabric.

To truly understand the trauma of the Black Man in America, we must confront the uncomfortable truths that lie beneath the surface. We must acknowledge the systemic barriers that have hindered his progress, the generational trauma that continues to burden his spirit, and the daily struggles he might face; it is not enough to recognize the pain and suffering. We must also celebrate the resilience, strength, and triumphs of the Black Man in America. We must uplift his success stories and contributions to the arts, sciences, politics, and every facet of society. We must embrace his cultural richness and diversity, recognizing that it is a source of strength and inspiration for the nation.

In the following chapters, we will explore the multifaceted experiences of the American Black man and the trauma he endures. We will probe into the historical context, the social and cultural challenges, and the ongoing fight for justice and equality. Through these stories, we hope to shed light on the resilience, strength, and unwavering spirit of the Black man in America. Through understanding and compassion, we can begin to heal the wounds of the past, dismantle oppressive systems, and forge a path toward a future where every Black man in America can truly thrive. We will delve deeper into the multifaceted experiences of the Black Man in America. We will explore the historical context, the social and cultural challenges, and the ongoing fight for justice and equality. Through these stories, we hope to open your eyes to understanding the depth of the Black man's trauma while highlighting the resilience and unwavering spirit that sustains him.

Through understanding, empathy, and a commitment to change, we can begin to trek forward to heal the wounds inflicted upon the Black Man in America. Through collective action and a shared belief in the inherent worth of every individual, we can dismantle the systems of oppression and create a society that honors and uplifts the Black Man in all his complexity. The trauma of the Black Man in America runs deep, but so does his strength, resilience, and unwavering determination to forge a future where true equality reigns. Together, let us embark on this journey as we strive to create a more just, inclusive, and compassionate America for all.

■■

CHAPTER 4

WHERE DOES THE BLACK MAN FIT IN AMERICAN SOCIETY

Where does the Black man fit in American Society?

The question of where the Black man fit in American society has been contentious since the country's founding. Enslaved Black people in the late 1800s as property rather than human beings even after slavery ended in the United States of America on December 6, 1865; black people continued to face discrimination, segregation, and violence at the hands of white Americans. Despite decades of progress, Black men in America still face significant challenges in finding their place in society; these men are more likely to be incarcerated, more likely to be victims of police brutality, and more likely to live in poverty than their white counterparts. Disparities have made many Black men feel like outsiders in their country, struggling to find a sense of belonging and purpose. One of the most significant challenges facing Black men in America is the criminal justice system. Black men are more likely to be arrested, convicted, and sentenced to a more lengthy prison term than white men for the same crimes; this disparity is partly due to systemic prejudices within the criminal justice system, which disproportionately targets Black people.

For many Black men, encounters with the police are fraught with danger. Black men must constantly be aware of their surroundings and behavior, knowing that even a minor infraction might lead to a violent confrontation with law enforcement. The fear of being stopped and harassed by police is a constant source of stress and anxiety for many Black men; it has significantly impacted their mental and emotional well-being. At forty-eight, a black man, who shall remain nameless, mentioned in an interview on May 17, 2023, that staying alive was his most tremendous success in the United States of America. The Black man here is not too far removed from the Clinton Administration's Law Enforcement strategy, which coined the "Stop and Frisk" Era in 1999 and onward.

Another significant challenge facing Black men is the ever-moving goalpost of economic opportunity. Black men have an inherited system of government that has set a course to alienate blacks in the previous years of the 2000s, which led to a higher risk of black men living in the poverty window, more than any other demographic group in America. To dive deeper is partly due to the legacy of racial bias in U.S. laws and segregation, which denied Black people access to education and job opportunities. Even with affirmative action and other policies designed to promote equality, Black men still face significant barriers to economic success.

Despite these challenges, many Black men in the U.S. work to find their place in society; these men are starting businesses, pursuing education, and advocating for social justice and equality. Black men are building communities and creating support networks to help each other overcome obstacles. Ultimately, the question of where the Black man fits in American society is a question that the community has identified. We must confront the legacy of discrimination that has shaped the United States of America's history and work to create a more equitable society. Only then can Black men genuinely find their place in America, free from the trauma and pain of systemic oppression.

CHAPTER 5

FAMILY - A JUXTAPOSITIONAL REALITY

Family, an institution revered and cherished worldwide, holds a complex and multifaceted reality for the Black man in the U.S.; it is a space of fortitude and trauma, love and struggle, strength and vulnerability. To truly understand the impact of family on the Black man's experience, we must navigate the intricacies of these juxtapositional realities. In one sense, family is an anchor, a source of unwavering support and love; within the confines of the familial embrace, the Black man finds solace, encouragement, and a sense of belonging. Family becomes a refuge from the external world, a haven of cultural traditions, values, and stories passed down through generations. The bonds forged within the Black family unit are often unbreakable, generating a collective strength that sustains them through the darkest times.

However, this image of familial harmony juxtaposes Black families' daily realities. The trauma experienced by the Black man extends its reach into the very fabric of family life. Fear of violence, the threat of systemic gender intolerance, and the pervasive sense of vulnerability cast a shadow over the black family unit. Many parents strive to protect their children from the harsh realities of a world that often sees blacks as threats rather than innocent beings; this burden weighs heavily on the Black man's psyche as he grapples with the responsibility of shielding his loved ones from a society that too often fails to acknowledge the black man's humanity.

Racial injustice's historical and ongoing impact also shapes the Black man's experience within the family unit. The legacy of servitude and segregation has left an imprint on the collective psyche of Black families, affecting their relationships, aspirations, and opportunities. The generational trauma cannot be understated, as it reverberates through the lives of Black men, influencing their self-perception, grit, and ability to navigate a world that often seeks to diminish their worth.

Furthermore, the complexities of family dynamics among relatives compound the structural challenges faced by Black communities. Economic disparities, limited access to quality education and healthcare, and systemic bigotry create additional obstacles for the Black man and his family; these external forces strain familial bonds as they navigate the delicate balance between survival and maintaining a sense of unity and love. Despite the challenges, Black families remained flexible, finding continued vulnerability and strength in their collective history and shared experiences; they celebrate their triumphs, support one another through adversity, and pass down a legacy of backbone and determination. Within the crucible of family, the Black man often finds the heart and fortitude necessary to confront the traumas inflicted upon him.

The reality of family for the Black man in America is a juxtaposition of love, struggle, strength, and vulnerability. He might find solace and support within the familial embrace while grappling with the weight of historical and modern trauma. The complex realities of family bonds exist alongside the broader social context in which he lives. Recognizing and understanding these complexities is crucial to comprehend the full impact of the trauma experienced by the Black man and his family.

CHAPTER 6

WHOLENESS - EXPLORING THE TOGETHERNESS OF THE AMERICAN SPIRIT

In the tapestry of American history, the Black man's experience knitted intertwined yet often overlooked, leaving behind a trail of untold stories and silenced voices. The trauma he endures in America is a deep wound that seeps into the very fabric of his existence, but amidst the pain and struggle, there exists a vehement spirit that seeks to find wholeness, to bridge the gap between the fractured pieces of his identity and the togetherness of the American spirit. The journey towards wholeness begins with acknowledging the complex and multilayered experiences of the Black man. The trauma, passed down through generations, has shaped his identity and left lasting scars on his soul. Yet, in the face of these complexities, he refuses to be defined solely by his pain. He yearns for a sense of belonging, a place where his story is accepted, respected, and woven into the tapestry of the American narrative.

The togetherness of the American spirit lies in recognizing that the Black man's struggle is not an isolated one but a shared burden; it requires empathy, understanding, and a willingness to confront the uncomfortable truths that have perpetuated inequality. Togetherness demands a collective effort to dismantle the structures that perpetuate and hinder the full realization of the American dream for all its citizens. To achieve wholeness, we must not erase or diminish the Black man's unique experiences; it is not about assimilation or conformity but embracing the richness of diversity and celebrating each individual's contributions to the table. In this tapestry of voices, cultures, and perspectives, the true essence of the American spirit thrives.

The Black man's stories, struggles, and triumphs must be acknowledged and integrated into the national narrative to foster wholeness, proper understanding, and empathy as yet cultivated through education, media representation, and the amplification of marginalized voices. The togetherness of the American spirit lies in the collective responsibility to dismantle the barriers that divide us; it requires introspection, self-awareness, and an unwavering commitment to justice and equality. The essence of national wholeness necessitates challenging our biases, dismantling systems of privilege, and embracing the discomfort of confronting our complicity in perpetuating injustice.

Achieving wholeness is not solely the responsibility of the Black man; it is a shared journey in which allies and advocates play a crucial role. As a nation in solidarity, allyship, and active anti-racist work, the togetherness of the American spirit boasts realization. As the journey toward wholeness unfolds, the Black man realizes he is not alone. He stands alongside countless others committed to dismantling systemic partiality, healing the wounds of the past, and creating a more just society. In his quest for wholeness, he finds strength in the collective power of those who believe in the transformative potential of the American spirit. Wholeness is an integral part of the journey toward healing the trauma of the Black man in America; it requires a collective effort to integrate the Black man's experiences into the American narrative. Empathy, understanding, and active engagement can bridge the gap between fractured identities and cultivate a sense of belonging and wholeness for all.

CHAPTER 7

A GRAPPLE WITH AMERICAN CRIME

The American rule of law is both a cornerstone and a safeguard of the nation, premised upon the consent of the governed; it is a boundary, setting the parameters within which justice should dispense. Lady Justice, blindfolded and holding scales, symbolizes the impartiality and fairness that should guide the judicial system. However, for the Black man in America, this idealistic vision often remains elusive, shattered by the pervasive trauma inflicted by a system meant to protect and serve.

In theory, the American rule of law should be indiscriminate, treating all individuals with equal respect, dignity, and protection. In practice, the experiences of Black men in America reveal a starkly different reality. The scales of justice seem tipped against him, heavily weighted by systemic prejudices and bias. The trauma endured is not merely a consequence of individual experiences but a consequence of a deeply entrenched structural flaw that perpetuates inequality.

Historically, the American justice system draws upon a marred remnant of slavery, segregation, and systematic oppression, the trauma inflicted upon the Black man intertwined with a long history of racial characterization, police brutality, and unequal treatment within the criminal justice system. The presumption of innocence considered a fundamental principle, often seems like an elusive mirage for Black men who are disproportionately targeted, vilified, and presumed guilty solely based on skin pigment color. The trauma of the Black man in America goes beyond the individual instances of injustice and brutality; it is a daily grapple with the pervasive fear of being wrongfully accused, unfairly treated, or even losing one's life at the hands of those sworn to protect and serve. Black men carry this weight throughout their lives, impacting their mental and emotional well-being and limiting their sense of safety and freedom.

The trauma activates by the lack of accountability and the perpetuation of systemic injustices. Too long have cases of police misconduct or excessive force been met with minimal consequences, perpetuating a cycle of mistrust and anger within Black communities. Failing to hold those responsible accountable erodes faith in the justice system, leaving many feeling abandoned and marginalized. Systemic change to address the trauma of the Black man in America is imperative; it requires a comprehensive examination of policing practices, sentencing disparities, and the broader criminal justice system. Restructuring the criminal justice system necessitates dismantling systemic racism that permeates facets of society, from education to employment opportunities, ensuring equal access to justice for all.

Furthermore, a real grapple with U.S. crime calls for a collective reckoning with the historical injustices that have shaped the present reality. Trauma will not heal without admission of the deeply ingrained biases and prejudices perpetuating inequality. Reimagining the American rule of law requires the active participation of all citizens, challenging the status quo and demanding a more just and compassionate society.

The trauma endured by the Black man in America directly results from a justice system that fails to uphold the principles it claims to represent. The American rule of law must evolve to become a proper safeguard for all, irrespective of race. Only then can we start to heal the wounds inflicted by centuries of systemic oppression and offer a genuine sense of justice and prosperity to every individual, regardless of the color of their skin.

∎∎

CHAPTER 8

GOVERNMENTAL LAW - A MOMENTOUS COMPARISON OF LAWS AFFECTING BLACK MEN

Specific laws in America have significantly impacted the lives of Black men in America. By drawing a momentous comparison between laws that have positively and negatively affected Black men, we aim to shed light on the systemic challenges they face within the legal framework; this chapter explores the historical context, legal disparities, and the long-lasting trauma inflicted on Black men by governmental laws. By examining specific regulations, we can better understand the complex relationship between legislation and the experiences of Black men in America.

The Civil Rights Act of 1964 was a positive law that paved the way for progress, which was pivotal in dismantling legalized segregation and discrimination; this groundbreaking legislation outlawed racial discrimination in employment, public accommodations, and education, among other areas. The Act provided Black men with increased opportunities for advancement, equal treatment, and protection under the law; its passage marked a significant step towards addressing and promoting equality. The Voting Rights Act of 1965 petitioned to remove barriers that prevented Black men from exercising their right to vote. By eliminating discriminatory practices such as literacy tests and poll taxes, this act sought to ensure equal access to the voting booth. For Black men, this legislation marked a crucial turning point in their ability to participate fully in the democratic process, empowering them to have a voice in shaping their communities and advocating for change.

Hostile laws perpetuating injustice and inequality were the War on Drugs and Mandatory Minimum Sentencing. The implementation of the War on Drugs, particularly during the 1980s and 1990s, disproportionately impacted Black men.

Draconian sentencing laws, such as mandatory minimums, resulted in severe penalties for non-violent drug offenses, leading to the overrepresentation of Black men in the criminal justice system; this approach perpetuated systematic discrimination, contributing to the mass incarceration crisis and further exacerbating the trauma experienced by Black men and their communities.

Stand Your Ground laws, which exist in several states, have disproportionately impacted Black men; these laws allowed individuals to use deadly force when they perceive a threat without a duty to retreat. Studies have shown that these laws have a racial bias, with Black men being more likely to face deadly consequences when confronted by individuals who invoke Stand Your Ground defenses; these laws perpetuate a climate of danger for Black men, further deepening their trauma and eroding their sense of safety. "Governmental Law: A Momentous Comparison of Laws Affecting Black Men" reveals the complexities inherent in the legal system's impact on the lives of Black men in America. While some laws, such as the Civil Rights Act and the Voting Rights Act, have advanced equality and empowered Black men, others, like the War on Drugs and Stand Your Ground laws, have perpetuated systemic injustice and deepened the trauma experienced by Black men. Recognizing the profound impact of governmental regulations on Black men is essential for dismantling systemic discrimination, advocating for equitable legislation, and healing the traumas that persist within these communities. We can strive towards a more just and inclusive society by addressing the disparities and rectifying the injustices.

■■

CHAPTER 9

EQUAL JUSTICE UNDER THE LAW

The long-awaited pursuit of justice for Black men in America is nigh; this groundbreaking discussion aims to shed light on the historical challenges and systemic disparities within the U.S. legal system that have perpetuated trauma within the Black community. We seek to understand the concept of justice and the transformative changes necessary to create a society where justice truly encompasses all. To comprehend the trauma experienced by Black men in America, we must own the historical context in which the legal system has operated. From the days of slavery to Jim Crow laws, the very foundation of the justice system has racial bias, discrimination, and inequality; these deeply ingrained biases have led to countless miscarriages of justice, perpetuating trauma within the Black community for generations.

The principle of "Equal Justice Under the Law" is a bedrock of the American legal system. However, this promise has been elusive for Black men for far too long. Despite constitutional guarantees, the reality of equal justice remains out of reach. Systemic biases, racial profiling, and over-policing have created an environment where Black men are disproportionately targeted, arrested, and incarcerated. The trauma inflicted upon them by a system that fails to provide equal protection under the law is profound and enduring. Addressing the trauma of Black men begins with comprehensive police reform. Transformative changes leading to a path to justice include implementing unbiased policing practices, increasing accountability, and establishing community-led oversight boards. Investing in de-escalation training, implicit bias training, and diversifying law enforcement agencies can help rebuild trust and create a more just system.

Reforming sentencing practices is essential to rectify the racial disparities that have plagued the criminal justice system. Mandatory minimums sentencing, three-strikes laws, and harsh sentencing guidelines disproportionately affect Black men, leading to excessive and unjust punishments. Implementing fair sentencing policies, such as alternatives to incarceration, restorative justice programs, and judicial discretion, can help restore balance and promote equitable outcomes. Addressing systemic racism at its core; requires dismantling institutional barriers perpetuating racial disparities, biases, and unequal treatment within the legal system. Investing in education, healthcare, and economic opportunities in marginalized communities can help break the cycle of trauma and create a more peace-driven society because there is an urgent need for transformative change within the legal system to address the life experience of Black men in America. We call you to action, urging individuals, communities, and policymakers to create a lawful procedure that upholds the promise of equal justice and helps heal the deep wounds that have long afflicted the Black community.

CHAPTER 10

INFLECTION POINT - NAVIGATING THE TURNING TIDE OF TRAUMA AND HOPE

We as a society are now at an inflection point that delves into a critical juncture in the trajectory of the Black man in America—a moment of immense trauma and undeniable expectation; it explores the evolving landscape of racial injustice, the catalysts that have brought us to this pivotal point, and the potential for transformative change; this chapter examines the challenges the Black community faces, the collective response to injustices, and the steps necessary to navigate this inflection point toward a more equitable and just future. To comprehend the present situation, we must understand the deep-rooted trauma experienced by the Black man in America. Generations of racial oppression, violence, and discrimination have left an indelible impact on our collective minds. The trauma manifests in various forms, including psychological distress, intergenerational trauma, and constant probable fear of being targeted or marginalized; we must seek to illuminate the multifaceted nature of this trauma, acknowledging its profound impact on the mental, emotional, and physical well-being of Black men while also recognizing their resilience and strength moving the needle forward toward an inflection point.

An inflection point does not emerge in isolation of the Black man; it is an unearthing catalyst arising from a confluence of events and triggers that compel society to confront its ingrained biases and injustices, which examines pivotal moments in recent history, such as the Black Lives Matter (BLM) movement, the murder of George Floyd, and the widespread protests against police brutality. Events such as these have motivated a broader awakening, prompting a reckoning with systemic racism and an urgent demand for change. By understanding these goads, we gain insight into the factors that have propelled us toward this inflection point. Our humanistic inquisition is to delve into the defining moments in recent history that have accelerated the trajectory toward change for the Black man in America. By examining specific dates and events, such as the Black Lives Matter (BLM) movement, the murder of George Floyd, Breonna Taylor, Tamir Rice, and the widespread protests against police brutality, we aim to understand how these pivotal moments have contributed to the current inflection point; the impact of these incidents, the collective response they inspired, and the potential for transformative change.

The Black Lives Matter (BLM) movement emerged in counter to the acquittal of Trayvon Martin's killer in 2013; it gained momentum and national attention succeeding the untimely death of Eric Garner in New York City, New York, and Michael Brown in Ferguson, Missouri in 2014. The movement, rooted in the fight against police violence, has galvanized millions nationwide and has become a powerful force demanding justice, accountability, and equal treatment for Black individuals. The BLM movement has significantly shaped public discourse and mobilized communities, making it a crucial turning point for change.

George Floyd's murder in May 2020, a Black man, at the hands of a Minneapolis police officer ignited a global outcry against police brutality and racial injustice. The horrific incident, captured on video, showcased the callousness and disregard for Black lives within law enforcement. Floyd's death sparked widespread protests across the United States and worldwide, demanding an end to police violence. The immense public outrage and the power of social media spotlighted the urgent need for change and propelled the fight for justice to new heights.

The shooting death of Breonna Taylor in March 2020, a young Black woman, by police officers in Louisville, Kentucky, further amplified the call for justice. Taylor's killing during a flawed and controversial raid on her apartment intensified public scrutiny of police tactics and highlighted the disproportionate violence faced by Black communities. Her case, alongside George Floyd's, became a rallying point for advocates seeking an end to police brutality, demanding accountability for those responsible, and pushing for systemic reforms within law enforcement agencies. To fully grasp the magnitude of the inflection point, we must acknowledge the countless Black lives of Akai Gurley, Tamir Rice, and Countless others: lost to police violence and racial injustice. Akai Gurley, an unarmed Black man, was fatally shot by a police officer in a New York City housing project 2014. Tamir Rice, a 12-year-old Black boy, was tragically killed by police in Cleveland, Ohio, while amusing himself with a toy gun in 2014, and many other incidents have contributed to the collective trauma experienced by the Black community and have further fueled the demand for it to end and the overhaul of policing practices.

The widespread protests against Police Brutality in 2020 after the murders of George Floyd, Breonna Taylor, and others, the United States witnessed an unprecedented wave of protests against flawed police practices and racial injustice; these protests, organized by diverse groups of activists, allies, and community members, transcended geographic boundaries and united people from all walks of life. The demonstrations became a global movement, echoing the demands for justice and prompting critical conversations about the urgent need for systemic change. The widespread protests have amplified the unheard's voices and become a powerful motivation for change.

At this inflection point, the power of collective response becomes increasingly evident. The mobilization and unity within the Black community and the crucial alliances formed with individuals and groups from diverse backgrounds highlight the importance of solidarity, and intersectionality in dismantling phycological racism and advancing social justice. By examining the strategies, protests, and advocacy efforts employed, we can appreciate the transformative potential of collective action in effecting change. In the face of this inflection point, it is essential to chart a path forward that recognizes the trauma and seizes the opportunities for progress. We must administer key steps necessary to navigate this critical moment, emphasizing the need for comprehensive reforms, including changes to legislation, law enforcement practices, educational curricula, and economic policies; it also underscores the importance of fostering dialogue, empathy, and understanding between communities, as well as investing in healing and restorative justice practices.

An inflection point serves as a compass, guiding us through the tumultuous waters of trauma and hope; it invites us to confront the deep-seated trauma experienced by the Black man in America while recognizing its power to propel us toward meaningful change. By understanding the impetus, mobilizing collective response, and navigating the path forward, we can create a future that upholds the inherent dignity, equality, and humanity of every Black man in America.

■■

CHAPTER 11

BLACK HERITAGE

Black Heritage has a rich cultural tapestry and shared experiences of Black people across the globe. By examining the connections between Native Americans, indigenous Black people of America, and other Black communities worldwide, we aim to highlight the deep-rooted heritage and collective resilience that unifies these diverse groups; this chapter explores the historical, cultural, and social ties that bind these communities, emphasizing the significance of Black heritage in shaping identities and fostering a sense of belonging. The history of Native or Indigenous Americans and Black people in America intertwines in a complex and often overlooked manner. The forced migration of enslaved individuals to the Americas brought different Black ethnic groups into contact with various black and brown indigenous tribes, leading to intercultural exchanges and the blending of traditions. Some Native American tribes, such as the Cherokee, Choctaw, and Seminole, embraced and integrated Black individuals into their communities, leading to a distinct group known as Black Indians or Afro-Indigenous people; these individuals, with their unique heritage, serve as a testament to the interconnectedness of Native American and Black cultures.

Within the United States, a long-standing community of indigenous Black people disappeared in the back-most part of the American psyche and mainstream narratives; these individuals, often referred to as Gullah Geechee or Maroon communities, are descendants of possible once enslaved individuals who established independent settlements in regions such as the Sea Islands of South Carolina and Georgia. The Gullah Geechee culture, characterized by vibrant traditions, a distinct language, and a solid connection to the land, showcases the resilience and resourcefulness of these communities. Recognizing and celebrating their heritage is crucial to understanding the diverse experiences of Black people in America.

Beyond the borders of the United States, Black people worldwide share a common heritage that transcends national boundaries. The African or Black diaspora has spread African or Black culture and traditions to various continents due to transatlantic travel and subsequent migrations. Black heritage's resilience and cultural richness are evident from the Afro-Caribbean communities in the Caribbean islands to the Afro-Brazilian and Afro-Colombian communities in Latin America; these communities have preserved and adapted African traditions, creating vibrant expressions of identity and pride.

One of the most potent mediums for preserving and celebrating Black heritage is through music, art, and language. From the critically acclaimed negro spirituals of the Black generations of old in America to the reggae music of Jamaica, the rhythms and melodies created by Black musicians have resonated across the globe, serving as a powerful unifying force. Visual art, such as the vibrant paintings of Haitian artists or the intricate beadwork of Native American and African artisans, reflects the shared experiences and cultural exchange between these communities. Additionally, preserving Afro-African languages, such as Gullah, Creole, and various indigenous languages, is a testament to the determination to maintain cultural identity and heritage.

Black Heritage, connecting Native Americans, Indigenous Black People of America, highlight the interconnectedness of Black communities worldwide. By exploring the ties between Native Americans, indigenous Black people of America, and other Black populations, we gain a deeper understanding of the resilience, cultural richness, and shared experiences that unite these communities. Acknowledging and celebrating this heritage is essential in fostering a sense of belonging, promoting cultural preservation, and advancing the collective pia of affinity.

■■

CHAPTER 12

RECOMPENSE

The trauma of the Black man in America is an undeniable reality, a deep-rooted wound that has festered for far too long. In pursuing justice, equality, and healing, addressing the importance of recompense is essential, delving into the significance of tangible and intangible reparations to address the historical and ongoing injustices inflicted upon the Black community. Recompense, in its most tangible form, encompasses financial compensation, the acknowledgment of past wrongs, and a commitment to rectifying the systemic inequalities that have plagued Black lives for centuries; it is a recognition that the Black man in America has endured unimaginable suffering, bearing the weight of servitude, segregation, discrimination, and institutionalized racism. To comprehend the necessity of recompense, one must confront the painful legacy of servitude; in some cases, it was a brutal and dehumanizing institution that stripped Black individuals of their humanity, freedom, and dignity. The repercussions of this dark period in American history reverberate through generations, perpetuating a cycle of disadvantage and damage that haunts Black communities today.

Recompense demands that we admit the economic disparities resulting from servitude and its aftermath. The wealth gap between Black and White Americans is not an accident but a consequence of deliberate policies and practices that hinder Black progress; it is a stark reminder that true equality abounds by rectifying the economic injustices inflicted upon the Black community. Recompense goes beyond mere financial reparations; it requires a commitment to dismantling the perpetual class disparities, such as unequal access to quality education, healthcare, housing, and employment opportunities. Restitution demands that we address the structural racism embedded in our institutions, ensuring every Black man in America has an equal chance to thrive and succeed.

Furthermore, recompense necessitates genuine reckoning with racial trauma's psychological and emotional toll. The Black man in America has experienced generational trauma, carrying the weight of countless acts of violence, discrimination, and oppression. To heal these deep wounds, we must prioritize mental health support, provide culturally competent care, and create safe spaces for healing and restoration. Recompense is not a handout but an acknowledgment of the debt owed to the Black community; it is an investment in a more just and equitable future for all. By providing reparations, we begin to rectify the injustices that have hindered the progress of Black individuals and communities. We confess the immense contributions of the Black man in America and seek to restore the nobleness taken from him. In embracing the concept of recompense, we acknowledge the collective responsibility we bear as a society; it is not enough to recognize the past; we must actively work towards a future where every Black man in America can flourish without the burden of classism, discrimination, and oppression. Recompense is an essential step toward healing, justice, and reconciliation; it is an opportunity for America to confront its painful history, learn from it, and strive for a more compassionate and equitable society. Only through genuine efforts to address the traumatization of the Black man in America can we hope to build a future where justice and equality prevail.

In the economic dimension, we must address the persistent wealth gap between Black and White U.S. citizens; it acknowledges that the economic disparities faced by the Black man in America are not accidental. Tangible reparations, such as financial compensation, investment in Black-owned businesses, and access to capital, are essential to rectify this imbalance. By providing economic opportunities and resources, we can dismantle the barriers hindering economic advancement in Black communities.

The social dimension of recompense acknowledges the need to rectify the social inequalities that have plagued the Black community for far too long; it involves investing in education, healthcare, housing, and employment opportunities in predominantly Black neighborhoods and communities. By dismantling discriminatory policies within the sectors, as mentioned earlier, we can ensure that every Black man in America has access to the same opportunities and resources as their counterparts.

The cultural dimension of recompense recognizes the importance of preserving and celebrating the rich cultural heritage of the Black community; it involves supporting and promoting Black artists, writers, musicians, and cultural institutions, ensuring that their contributions are recognized and valued. Cultural reparations also entail challenging and dismantling cultural appropriation and stereotypes perpetuating harmful narratives about Black men in America. By embracing and uplifting Black culture, we foster a more comprehensive society that honors all its members' diverse experiences and contributions.

The dimensions of recompense are interconnected and integral to addressing the injury of the Black man in America. By examining the economic, social, and cultural aspects of reparations, we can begin dismantling the oppression systems that have perpetuated racial inequalities; through these comprehensive efforts, we can strive towards true healing for the Black community.

■■

CHAPTER 13

HUMAN CONSCIOUSNESS IS RISING

Boastful and free is he who dares to dream of an America where every American boy hastens to tread upon the sacred ground of equality and justice. In the depths of his consciousness, the Black man envisions a nation where the seeds of countenance are sown and nurtured among a decent civilization, basking in the bounty of irrefutable freedom; this vision, born out of an indomitable spirit, resonates deeply within the American consciousness. Throughout history, the American nation has stood as a testament to the valor and heroism of those who fought for justice and equality. The collective strength of a country that has revered the flags of justice exemplifies the triumphs achieved. The journey westward, guided by the celestial stars, symbolizes a quest for liberty, where the American spirit galloped forward, settling and shaping a land that embraces the beauty of diversity. The Black man, with wide-eyed wonder, recognizes that his home lies at the river of running water, where a nation is grounded, molded, and blessed by his presence.

However, once a torch that forever burned brightly, the American way has sometimes faltered, casting shadows of discord and dissent. The rise of a rightist ideology threatens the progress made by the Black man and challenges the essence of his American dream. What has become of this rightist movement that moves forward with its agenda, circumventing the fundamental principles upon which this nation builds?

The Black man, as the keeper of the nation's progress, acknowledges the complexities of this moment. The realization dawns within the depths of his mind - that our human consciousness is rising. The legacy of struggle and perseverance has birthed a collective awakening as people from all walks of life join hands to dismantle the barriers that impede progress and equitability.

The Black man, with hardihood and determination, becomes a stimulant for change. He recognizes that the fight for justice is not limited to his community but a discourse encompassing all who yearn for a society founded on equality and respect. The rising human consciousness transcends race, creed, and background as individuals unite to pursue a more just and equitable America.

In this moment of awakening, the Black man understands the power of unity and the need for solidarity. He acknowledges that the fight for justice is not an isolated struggle but a collective effort to dismantle the systems of oppression that hinder progress. Together, voices rise, demanding change and holding the U.S. accountable for its promise of liberty and justice. As the collective human consciousness increases, the Black man stands at the precipice, leading the charge toward a brighter future. In his stride, he carries the weight of generations past, fueled by the hope that his children and grandchildren will inherit an America that cherishes their worth and acknowledges their contributions.

The rising human consciousness catalyzes change in America. The Black man, in his quest for humanistic value, embodies the spirit of vim and determination. Together, united by a shared vision of a better future, people from all backgrounds join forces to tear down the barriers that divide us. The journey towards a more just and unprejudiced America requires the collective effort of all who believe in the power of unity and the promise of a nation that fulfills its ideals.

CHAPTER 14

AMERICAN CLOSURE

How would one close the chapter of the Black man's pain in the gazes of a nation being reborn? The Black man has awakened to a tremulous American dream that, with glaring eyes, includes him. How does the Black man thrive in an American system designed to deter the Black soul from even the thoughts of fitting in - let alone securing American ideals, freedom and rights that belong to every true-hearted American? The Black man gleams gleefully at the view of achieving success in Her lady's stretched water-bound west and eastern borders of a new country Western caricature. I say now that the Black man is in a constant battle to prove his worthiness of a countenance and in an even greater struggle to assert his prowess as a staple being of American society.

As the years are troth waning into a state of perpetual pressing of the olive - the Black man has managed to garner American society's reflectivity as he takes strides forward to debase and assert his browned soul hastening to the American washboard in a constant attempt and surrender of his place in Americas' war-chest. The Black man is cemented in his geology in America's pocketbook with determined yet meek prowess as he jangles forward and is bound in a state of a future spent tally with his Black face glued into America's multifaceted soul. America's Black man is a movement and yet likened to causation that only his Black should carry out. The Black man has a determined destiny to monologue the American clock of destitute onward into the rising ambers of a hastening patriotism. The Black man, as he is here on American soil, grows in fortitude, and he marches ahead as would he bearing in the arm and leading an American code of nationalism. As he stands tall yet with moral regard for his stature - the Black man moves further inward as the American fabric of woven intricate ideals nudges his Blackness scrupulously to charge the American heel of the foot to hasten to the places that our nation is boastfully as much as to a presuppose dutifully as to heal the American Soul Nation.

An American Soul-Nation is the unspoken will of the American Soul to battle an estuary in a meaningful stream of American continence to once-and-for-all include the American Black man into the rotunda as a necessary part of American life. Herewith, is heralding the Nation's Black Man being now an American ideal of a sanctimonious nod to the heavens proudly beating with the heart Soul-Nation; the Black man exists - he acknowledged into the American Soul-Nation as a home plate as American strength of the American-Framework.

American closure is not just a closing of a chapter but a mending of a wound that has been open for far too long. American closure is a recognition that the Black man has endured trauma in America. Still, it is also a call to action for the nation to heal and move forward together - - acknowledging the pain and struggles that the Black man has faced while also uplifting him and recognizing his value as a vital member of American society.

The road to American closure is not an easy one, but it is one that we must all embark on together. The closure here is a willingness to confront the injustices and to work towards a more equitable future. The road to the Black man's stature requires listening to the voices of the Black community and taking action to address their concerns. The route requires a commitment to education, dialogue, and empathy.

As we work towards American closure, we must remember that the Black man is not a monolith. He is a complex and diverse group of individuals with unique experiences and perspectives. We must celebrate their differences and recognize the strength that comes from diversity. Ultimately, American closure is not just about closing a chapter; it is about opening a new one - creating a future where the Black man is not just included but celebrated. The United States of America's closure is about building a country that lives up to its ideals of freedom and equality for all.

■■

CHAPTER 15

GEORGE WASHINGTON'S WARNING TO THE STATE: UPHOLDING AMERICAN LIBERTY FOR ITS CITIZENS

In the annals of American history, the name George Washington stands tall as a founding father and the first President of the United States. His leadership and wisdom shaped the very foundation of this nation. However, buried within the legacy of this revered figure lies a warning, a cautionary tale that resonates deeply with the trauma faced by Black men in America.

Crucial is it to examine the ideals upon which the nation proves. The principles of liberty, justice, and equality were etched into the fabric of America's birth, promising a land of opportunity and freedom for all. Yet, George Washington recognized that some people only partially realized these ideals.

Washington delivered a powerful message to the American people in his farewell address. His words echoed through time, warning about the dangers of neglecting the duty to uphold American liberty solely for its citizens. Washington cautioned against favoring one group, urging unity and equality as the bedrock of a solid and prosperous nation.

However, the trajectory of history reveals a stark reality. The Trauma of the Black Man in America is deeply rooted in discrimination that has persisted throughout the centuries. From the brutality of slavery to the Jim Crow era and the ongoing struggle for civil rights, Black men have faced a distinct and enduring campaign to claim their rightful place in this nation.

The very notion of American liberty, as envisioned by Washington and other founding fathers, has often been a distant dream for Black men. Black men have encountered countless visible and invisible barriers that hinder their pursuit of life, liberty, and happiness. To truly address this trauma, it is imperative to confront the legacy of inequality and address America's failure to uphold its founded principles.

In the spirit of George Washington's warning, we must strive for a nation that upholds American liberty for all its citizens, regardless of race or ethnicity; it is a collective responsibility to dismantle the structures that perpetuate inequality and to foster an environment that allows every individual, including Black men, to flourish and reach their full potential; it is essential to understand the roots of this struggle and to work toward a society that embodies the values espoused by our founding fathers. Only then can we hope to heal the wounds inflicted by centuries of oppression and pave the way for a future where the trauma of the Black man becomes a distant memory, replaced by a narrative of resilience, equality, and true American liberty.

Made in the USA
Coppell, TX
17 November 2023